My Magical Unicorn
Coloring book for kids
DEDICATION
To all the kids and grown-ups that love drawing and coloring. Have fun coloring.
I0772659

This Book
Belongs To

Draw something

Draw something

Draw something

Draw something

Draw something

Draw something

Draw something

Draw something

Draw something

Draw something

Draw something

Draw something

Draw something

Draw something

Draw something

Draw something

Draw something

Draw something

Draw something

Draw something

Draw something

Draw something

Draw something

Draw something

Draw something

Draw something

Draw something

Draw something

Draw something

Draw something

Draw something

Draw something

Draw something

Draw something

Draw something

Draw something

Draw something

Draw something

Draw something

Draw something

Draw something

Draw something

Draw something

Draw something

Draw something

Draw something

Draw something

Draw something

Draw something

Draw something

Draw something

Draw something

Draw something

Draw something

Draw something

Draw something

Draw something

Draw something

Draw something

Draw something

Draw something

Draw something

Draw something

Draw something

Draw something

Draw something

Draw something

Draw something

Draw something

Draw something

Draw something

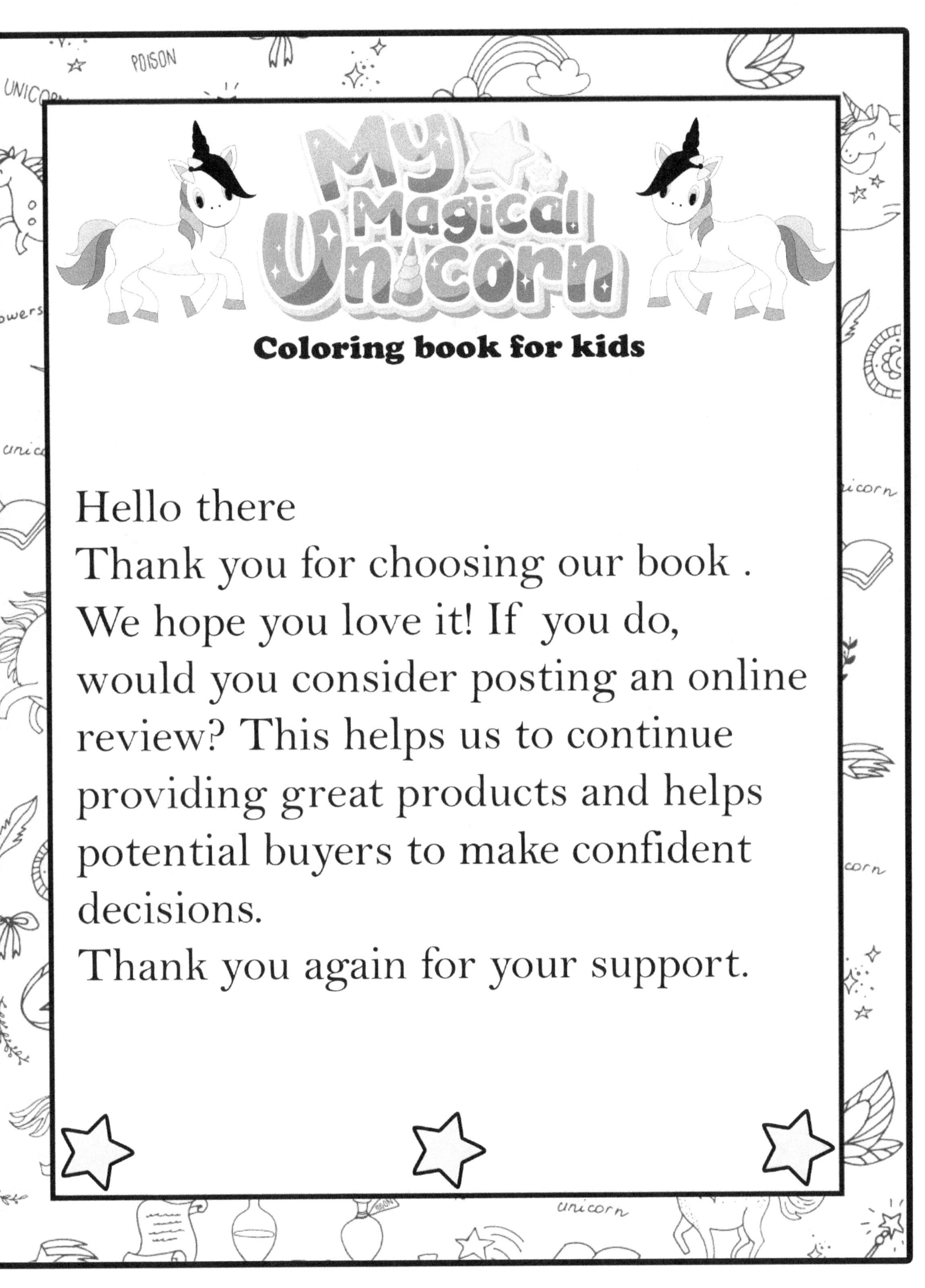

My Magical Unicorn

Coloring book for kids

Hello there

Thank you for choosing our book .

We hope you love it! If you do,
would you consider posting an online
review? This helps us to continue
providing great products and helps
potential buyers to make confident
decisions.

Thank you again for your support.

www.ingramcontent.com/pod-product-compliance
Lightning Source LLC
Chambersburg PA
CBHW081019260726
48662CB00025B/2410